THE LITTLE BOOK OF

Big Questions

200 WAYS TO EXPLORE YOUR SPIRITUAL NATURE

=== THE LITTLE BOOK OF ===

Big Questions

200 WAYS TO EXPLORE YOUR SPIRITUAL NATURE

Jonathan Robinson

Conari Press
Berkeley, California

Conari Press books are distributed by Publishers Group West
ISBN: 1-57324-014-1
Cover design by Christine Leonard Raquepaw

Library of Congress Cataloging-in-Publication Data
Robinson, Jonathan, 1959-
    The little book of big questions : 200 ways to explore your spiritual nature / by Jonathan Robinson.
        p. cm.
    Includes bibliographical refernces.
    ISBN 1-57324-014-1 (trade paper)
    1. Spiritual life—Miscellanea.   I. Title.
BL624.R623   1995
291.2—dc20   95-20442

Printed in the United States of America on recycled paper.
10 9 8 7 6 5 4 3

*To the infinite, spiritual essence in each of us,
and to my sweetheart, Helena.*

Acknowledgments

I want to thank Mary Jane Ryan at Conari Press for her enthusiasm and suggestions for enhancing this book. You're a delight to work with. My spiritual mentors, Justin and Joyce, were instrumental in having me pursue the questions in my soul and helped me persist enough to find some answers. I am ever indebted to both of you. With profound gratefulness, I thank the Creator of all for planting these questions in my head and giving me the people and experiences to nourish them properly. The music of John Astin has been like a gourmet meal for my hungry heart—thanks for your contribution. And, lastly, to my family and friends who have been greatly supportive of me and my spiritual pursuits.

TABLE OF CONTENTS

1

WHY ASK WHY, AND HOW TO DO IT

It is better to know some of the questions than all of the answers.
—James Thurber

Trying to have an intelligent and inspirational conversation about spirituality can be, well, trying. Case in point: For years, I tried to share with my dad some of my spiritual beliefs and experiences. For years, he, an avowed atheist, avoided such conversations. One day, I changed my approach. Instead of telling him about my beliefs, I simply asked him questions such as, "Have you ever had a really unusual or psychic experience?" and "What do you find to be mysterious or magical about life?" To my surprise, he had a lot to say. Soon we were fully engaged in a conversation about the wonders of the universe. In fact, after a while he was practically "preaching" to me about how life is so marvelously complex that there must be "something more than meets the eye" going on.

From this experience, I was able to share a whole new level of intimacy with my father. In addition, I was exposed to some fascinating ideas that had never occurred to me before. I quickly became hooked on the value of asking people profound questions about life's greatest mysteries.

I later realized that the questions I was asking others could be used as a tool to delve more deeply into my own beliefs, understandings, and experiences. I believe that everyone has a storehouse of wisdom inside them that usually goes untapped. By asking ourselves profound questions, it's possible to discover or uncover our own illuminating answers. I like to think of each of the questions in this book as an opportunity for us to experience a deeper, more enlightened level of consciousness. As we contact our innate inner wisdom, we can positively affect the course of our lives. By asking our friends and family to explore these questions with us, we can experience a deeper level of intimacy and support than ever before.

The magical thing about love is the more you give it away, the more you end up having. The same could be said about spiritual questions. The more you offer these questions to friends and family, the more you get back. In the past, most of us have yearned to explore these profound topics with others but have not known how to ask such things without appearing "weird." With this book in hand, you now have a "legitimate" reason to explore these topics. With an open mind and a sincere desire to learn, you'll find that nuggets of wisdom can be found in the answers of every person with whom you explore these ideas.

In recent years, people in the West have displayed a growing hunger for spiritual wisdom and experiences. With increasing age, we see the limitations of trying to find fulfillment in the material world. We come to understand that our time on Earth is short. We feel in our hearts a thirst for greater meaning and purpose and a desire to share a higher love with our kids, our family, and our friends. Yet, the means for deepening our spiritual lives has not always been clear.

Perhaps we can learn from the great advancements in science over the past hundred years. What has allowed technology to accelerate has been the ability of scientists to share their discoveries with like-minded researchers throughout the world. In the same way, as we share our spiritual questions, beliefs, and experiences with each other, perhaps a great leap forward can take place in human consciousness. By asking and exploring the "big questions" together, we can inspire each other to discover our own answers to life's greatest mysteries.

My own spiritual path has taken many unexpected twists and turns. As an agnostic sixteen year old, I experienced a sudden glimpse of "another world." The ecstasy and bliss I felt were so intense that I wrote in my journal, "ten seconds of this experience is worth a lifetime of effort." I began my intensive spiritual search the following day.

Over the years, I've been led to various mentors, teachers, and spiritual methods. I've traveled to twenty-seven countries, lived in three different spiritual communes, and taken countless retreats in search of greater spiritual understanding. Then, in 1992, I began interviewing many of the foremost spiritual leaders in the world, figuring that the best way to learn any subject is to ask experts for their best ideas and techniques. Their answers to the questions I asked them were compiled in a book titled, *Bridges to Heaven: How Well-Known Seekers Define and Deepen Their Connection with God.*

Because I interviewed such people as Mother Teresa, Marianne Williamson, Wayne Dyer, and Ram Dass for the *Bridges to Heaven* book, I would often be asked what it was like to talk with such notable people. Typically, I would say how each of the interviews glistened with a sense of the sacred. At first, I thought this was because of the caliber of the people I was talking with. Yet, in my interview with actor LeVar Burton (of *Roots* and *Star Trek* fame), he said something that gave me another point of view. I had asked him how he goes about contacting God, and he said, "You know, no one has ever asked me a question like that before. I think simply asking a question like that, and talking about these subjects, helps us to contact our essence."

Indeed, I've found that asking *anyone* questions that explore our essence can be an aid for letting Spirit manifest. Encouraging people to talk about how they open their heart is a way of getting a foot in the door of the world of the sacred. What we focus on grows. We just need the right stimulus (that is, the right questions) to help guide us in a beneficial direction. The fact that you have this book in your hand means you long for something beyond the ordinary in life. I hope you'll continue to use this book with friends, with family, and with yourself to keep the spiritual spark in you glowing.

How to Use This Book

There are four ways to answer the questions in this book. The first is to simply say the first response that comes to mind. This method is especially useful for becoming aware of what you've believed in the past. A second way is to allow yourself to open up to a quieter, more intuitive place within. When doing this, it can be helpful to repeat the question several times to yourself, then sit silently and listen for the still, small voice within. When you get an "Aha!"—a sense that an answer feels "right"—you've got the answer you were looking for. You can also play a special game: Try pretending you're a great, enlightened being who *knows* the answers to all of life's mysteries. The answers you come up with may very well surprise you.

A final way to use this book is in a loose, informal manner with friends or family. Asking people around the dinner table or at a discussion group a question from this book can begin a process of inquiry that can go anywhere you want it to go. Conversations based on these questions can be quite fascinating and can lead to a deeper level of friendship and understanding. If you have kids, you'll find that they also love to be asked the "big questions," and their answers may very well be surprising and profound.

As you read through this book, you'll find that some questions affect you much more deeply than others. Perhaps they bring up an issue you need to focus on at this point in your life, or they excite your imagination in new ways. It may be helpful to circle such questions in order to easily access them for further contemplation. In addition, many people find writing their answers in a journal to be useful for exploring these questions in greater depth.

You'll notice that amid the many questions in this book, I occasionally provide stories from my life. These anecdotes serve as an introduction to the question that follows. My hope is they will remind you of meaningful moments in your own life and stimulate you to think of new and creative ways of approaching each question.

The questions and reflections in this book are like a launching pad, and you are the rocket ship. The fuel to blast off into the cosmos is provided by your sincerity, wisdom, and imagination. Once you've launched yourself into one of the book's questions, feel free to let the conversation or reflection meander toward related ideas and questions. You're also invited to skip the questions or chapters you don't care for, and go with the ones that most excite you. Follow your bliss. Follow your curiosity. Follow your sense of wonder. Happy journeying.

2

WHO ARE YOU?

Life is a lot like football—if you want to be the Quarterback,
you first have to know where your Center is.
—Swami Beyondananda

Before commencing on any journey, it's good to first know where you currently are. The inquiries in this chapter include many of the most frequent "big questions" people have asked themselves throughout history. When athletes want to go to the next level of their sport, they frequently begin by mastering the fundamentals. You can consider the questions that follow as the fundamentals of spiritual exploration. The answers you come up with now will help lay a foundation for exploring ideas in more detail later on in the book.

Although these questions are of obvious importance, you may never have had an opportunity to tell someone your answers. You might be surprised to hear what you have to say on these topics. Unfortunately, in our consumer-oriented society, we're more likely to be asked, "Do you want fries with that?" than be asked, "What is the purpose of life?" You may feel resistance to tackling such big topics and personal issues, yet I'm sure you'll find it well worth your effort to persevere.

You may also find initial resistance to plunging into these topics when asking friends or family these questions. There's a tendency to want to stay with subjects we are fully accustomed to and comfortable with, rather than explore the unknown. Sometimes we even make fun of such questions, which allows us to avoid trying to answer them. However, if you display a sincere curiosity when asking others, you'll find there is a part in every person that yearns to explore these themes. That divine spark can be made to glow and catch fire if you can listen with a keen interest. In fact, asking people these important questions can be a great form of selfless service. It gives the people you care about an opportunity to reconsider the foundation on which they base their lives.

1. *What matters most in your life?*

2. *What do you think is the meaning or purpose of life?*

During my first trip to India, I went to visit a famous enlightened master known as Poonjaji. Poonjaji does not lecture. He only has one-on-one interactions with students while hundreds of people silently watch. One day he gestured for me to sit before him. After a minute of silence, he asked me a single question:

"Who are you?"

I innocently responded, "I'm Jonathan Robinson, from the United States."

Compassionately, Poonjaji said, "No, no, who are *YOU?*"

I didn't know what to say. Finally, I muttered, "I'm a soul."

Poonjaji shot back, "Show me soul."

Looking into his dancing eyes, I realized that *soul* was just an idea in my head, so I blurted out, "I'm an ego."

Once again, Poonjaji responded, "Show me ego."

I realized that *ego* was just *another* idea in my head, as were any other answers I might come up with. Sitting there, dropping all ideas of who I was and just being present with him, tears started streaming down my face. I suddenly felt as boundless as the sky.

Poonjaji gently said, "*Now* you *know* who you are."

3. Who are you?

4. What are the three most important things you've learned about life so far?

5. Do you think it pays to be a "good person," someone who is kind and fair? Why?

6. How can you know your higher destiny?

7. How happy or fulfilled are you at this time in your life?

8. What do you consider to be the difference between religion and spirituality?

9. What is your current notion of God? Would you say God to you is an indwelling spirit? A creator who is separate from us? A personal God? An impersonal energy? Who or what is God?

10. How do you differentiate guidance that comes from your ego from guidance that is divinely inspired?

When I was in college, my roommate, Tony, was the only freshman on the varsity basketball team. He was always envious of my grades, and I was always jealous of his athletic abilities. Whenever I'd come home with high grades, he'd jokingly say, "Before you start thinking you're hot stuff, let's play a game of one-on-one basketball."

After several months of this, I finally said to him, "Okay, I'm ready for a game of basketball on one condition: I get to bring a six-inch gadget onto the court and place it wherever I want." Tony was perplexed by my request, but was not going to miss a chance to put me in my place.

When we got to the court, I took out a blindfold and announced that this was my "six-inch gadget." I proceeded to place it in a very strategic location—over Tony's eyes. Then I said, "Let the games begin!"

Admittedly, the game still ended up being somewhat close. The final score was 20 to 12. Despite my lack of ability, I learned that if you make enough shots in the right direction, eventually something will go in the basket. It just goes to show you that to reach a goal, innate talent is not as important as defining exactly what you're aiming for.

11. What does spiritual growth mean to you? What is the "goal" of your spiritual pursuits?

12. What is love to you? What does it mean to give love to another person?

13. What do you think would help make you even happier and more fulfilled?

14. What currently brings you a real sense of joy?

15. What do you think will happen to you after you die?

16. How much time do you devote to spiritual practice and exploration per week?

A Meditation on "Who Are You?"

Behind the various roles we play and desires we have is a part of ourselves that could best be described as "pure awareness." In the course of our lives, we are always identifying with the latest sense of what we're doing and who we think we are: I'm a person reading a book; I'm a person in a hurry; I'm a parent, and so on.

This meditation is designed to help you go beyond all identifications and glimpse being the part of you that just "witnesses" life. When we become totally in the moment, free of all past or future ideas of who we are, we enter into a world where we are in the eternal present.

Sit in a comfortable chair, take a couple of deep breaths, and begin slowly and repetitively asking yourself the question: Who am I? If you prefer, you can ask the question: Who is in? Try to feel or sense how you are now, identifying with being a certain "somebody," such as someone who is trying a meditation exercise, or someone who is thinking about other things. As soon as you realize that you're caught up in a certain past or future identity, relax or let go of that sense of yourself and just *be* in the present moment. Soon you'll get caught up in more thoughts or a new identity. Once again, let the question, Who am I? or your sense of "me-ness" be a reminder to have you come back to the present moment and relax into pure awareness. Do this exercise for as long as you like. At first, don't be frustrated if you spend your whole time lost in thoughts. With practice, you'll get brief glimpses of pure, timeless awareness. Eventually, those moments can expand, and you'll realize that you are more than who you thought you were.

3

PERSONAL
SPIRITUAL HISTORY

The past does not have to equal the future.
—Anthony Robbins

When someone goes to a psychotherapist to make changes in their life, the sessions frequently begin with an exploration of their past. By understanding the past, one can better face the present with an increased level of wisdom. In the same way, as we review our unique *spiritual* past, we are better able to heal our "spiritual wounds" and face the future with more understanding.

To a large extent, you and I are a product of our childhood conditioning, yet when we see something in ourselves that we don't like, it's easy to feel guilty and ashamed. Likewise, when other people do things that annoy us, our compassion and tolerance can go right out the window. Exploring childhood roots of behavior can bring about an increased level of compassion. It becomes clearer why we behave the way we do and why others behave the way *they* do. As we become more aware of our conditioning, it's easier to break free of our limiting judgments and beliefs.

The questions that follow are for helping you to understand your unique spiritual history. As with all the questions in this book, you may wish to have a friend ask you the questions rather than simply answer them to yourself. Telling a friend about your childhood spiritual memories is tantamount to "spiritual psychotherapy." In some cases, answering these questions could bring up strong feelings, memories, and insights. Be willing to take the time you need to assimilate whatever thoughts or revelations arise.

1. *What was the very first notion of God you remember having as a child?*

2. *What did your parents directly or indirectly influence you to believe about God?*

3. *What religion, if any, do you identify with the most? Why?*

When I was about seven years old, I became intensely afraid of dying. I would lie awake and think about how I might die during the night and then be gone for all of eternity. Once I could take it no longer, I told my mom about my fears. My mother had always been skeptical about God, but at that moment I needed something to believe in. As I sobbed my fears to her, she compassionately explained that there was a prayer I could say to God that would help. The prayer was: "Now I lay me down to sleep, I pray to God my soul to keep. If I die before I wake, I pray to God my soul to take." That was the first prayer I ever said. And my prayer was answered in that my fears of dying disappeared. To this day, I pinpoint that moment with my "nonspiritual" mother as the beginning of my spiritual quest. Thanks, Mom.

4. *Did you pray as a child? Why or why not?*

5. *How are your spiritual beliefs similar to those of your parents?*

6. *How are your spiritual beliefs different from those of your parents?*

7. *How is your relationship with God similar to the relationship you had with your parents when you were young?*

8. What was the most negative experience you can remember as a child that affected how you view religion or spirituality?

9. What was the most positive experience you can remember as a child that affected how you view religion or spirituality?

10. Were you required to go to a religious school of some kind? If so, how did that impact how you felt about God and religion?

11. As a child, what were you led to believe would happen to you after you died?

One day when playing baseball with a bunch of friends, I hit my head on the ground when diving for a fly ball. Soon thereafter, I couldn't remember anything about who I was, where I was, or even my own name. Physically, I felt fine; I just didn't know anything about myself. As friends escorted me to the doctor's office, I asked them questions about myself. Because I felt no attachment to the person known as Jonathan, I asked very personal questions, such as: What am I normally like to be around? and, What are my strengths? What do you see as my weaknesses? It was fascinating to hear my friends answer these questions so honestly. Since I didn't identify (at the time) with being Jonathan, I was able to listen fully to what my friends had to say. Their feedback was extremely helpful in getting an accurate picture of myself from the viewpoint of others. Perhaps you can ask a trusted friend the same questions.

12. *What would you say are your spiritual weaknesses?*

13. *What have you considered to be your spiritual strengths?*

14. *As a child, what were you led to believe about other religions?*

15. *In your family and religion, what were you taught was God's way of viewing you when you "sinned" or did something "wrong"?*

16. *How has what you were led to believe about God when you were a child affected your relationship with God today?*

4

WHY DO YOU THINK . . .

Why have you come to Earth? Do you remember?
Why have you taken birth? Do you remember?
—John Astin

For many years, I was part of a group in which the leader would sometimes select a person to give a spontaneous forty-minute talk on spirituality. We never knew who was going to be chosen, so it made no sense to prepare beforehand. Whenever it was my turn, I would nervously stand up in front of the thirty or so people and just begin talking from my heart. I usually had no idea what I was going to say, but somehow it always ended up sounding surprisingly coherent and powerful. To the group's amazement, no matter who stood up to speak, great words of wisdom and inspiration would flow. From this experience, I realized that we are all a lot wiser than we're aware of consciously. If given a chance, we can tune in to a storehouse of inner wisdom.

With the questions in this chapter, you'll be given an opportunity to tap into your own storehouse of wisdom. Often, we doubt our understanding, and thereby fail to expound on the wisdom that could benefit ourselves and others. We look to "experts," such as priests, rabbis, or people who have written books to tell us what we already know in our soul. Yet when we begin to have faith in our own understanding, we can avoid the trap of always looking outside ourselves for answers to our own personal questions.

In one of Bill Cosby's early comedy albums, he does a skit in which he describes how, in college, he was dating a very intelligent woman who would frequently contemplate the question: Why is there air? Mr. Cosby, a physical education major at the time, thought the answer to the question was totally obvious: to blow up basketballs, to blow up volleyballs. As you can see from this example, questions can be answered at various levels. With each new level, questions can tune us in to a whole new perception of reality.

As you answer the questions in this chapter, you might try a couple of simple techniques for helping you tap into your innate wisdom. First, as suggested earlier, try pretending you're an enlightened being who really *knows* the answers to these questions. This can help you past any tendency you may have to doubt yourself. Second, try speaking for at least two or three minutes on each question. Even if you don't know what you're going to say, just keep talking. Don't try to quickly come up with the "correct" answer; rather, use each question as a catalyst for exploring deep spiritual and philosophical issues. Amid the trivial things you may say will be pearls of wisdom.

You may also choose to use these questions as a topic of discussion with family or friends. When doing this, simply ask the question of the entire group and see what each person says. Encourage people to speak from their heart—not to convince others of their point of view, but to share and develop their own wisdom. Allow silence to exist until you or others feel moved to speak. Sometimes, a very creative and thought-provoking interchange can occur by building on what other people in the group have said. Two heads are usually better than one, whereas five heads working in synchrony can have insights beyond anyone's expectations.

1. Why do you think the Bible is the bestselling book of all time?

2. Why did the Buddha proclaim that life is unsatisfactory and filled with suffering?

3. Why has Christmas been transformed from a religious holiday to one in which there is a big emphasis on buying presents?

4. Why have people of different religions historically argued over the right way to know God?

5. How has the rise of technology and material comforts affected our spiritual pursuits?

6. Why is it that 95 percent of Americans report that they believe in God, and yet our culture is so materialistic?

7. Why does our culture try to hide and avoid death as a reality in our lives?

The musical group Indigo Girls was playing in town, and I was thinking of going. I asked my intuition if I should, and got a strange message: You should go to the concert, but not pay for your own ticket. I thought that was crazy, but I had nothing else to do, so I went. Outside the gate, I saw a friend of mine, who quickly asked me if I had an extra ticket. I said no, and we got to talking. It turned out she didn't have any money, so she was asking everyone who passed by for a free ticket. I watched her admiringly. After several minutes, one young man said he had an extra ticket and offered to sell it to my friend for just ten dollars (it was a thirty-five-dollar ticket). She said she didn't have any money. My intuition clearly told me to buy the ticket for her, so I did. When I gave it to her, she was very grateful but resumed asking people for tickets. After a few more minutes, another person said he had an extra ticket. Once again, my friend mentioned that she had no money. This guy took out the ticket and just *gave* it to her. When he left, she passed the ticket on to me. The miracle was now complete. Sometimes the universe can be a mighty friendly place.

8. *Why do people in this culture rarely take the time to ask or listen to their intuition?*

9. *Why are some people born into an easy life whereas others are born into a life filled with suffering and abuse?*

10. Why do people often fail to do what's good for them (such as exercise, meditate, eat nutritious foods, and so on) and frequently do what harms their physical and spiritual health?

11. If you assume that there is a single God (or single Higher Power), why do you think there are so many different religious beliefs?

12. Why are books about spiritual topics selling so well now?

13. How has the disintegration of the traditional American family affected our spiritual pursuits?

For years, I had heard of the benefits of tithing (giving away 10 percent of your income to worthy causes). Proponents of tithing suggest that it is both spiritually and financially beneficial. Call it a lack of faith, but I had a hard time seeing how giving away money could be a financial benefit. Nevertheless, one year I decided to give it a try. Instead of sending checks to organizations and people I would never meet, I chose to try a new way of tithing. I bought about fifty dollars worth of ice cream and went down to the local beach with a sign that read, "Get FREE ice cream here." I figured, what better way to spread around some smiles than to give away ice cream?

At first, everyone was suspicious. My ice cream and I waited patiently for courage to prevail. Finally, a brave six-year-old girl came up to me and sweetly said, "How much is your free ice cream?" I gave her a double scoop. She was absolutely delighted. When watchful parents saw that the little girl didn't die from food poisoning, a steady stream of kids and parents made the pilgrimage to my little ice-cream stand.

As I busily scooped up smile after smile, parents repeatedly asked me why I was giving away ice cream. I would say, "I like to spread joy, and this is an easy way to do it."

Several parents asked me what I did for a living, and I reported I was a psycho-therapist and hypnotist. Four people asked me for my card, which I wasn't carry-ing, but I gave them my phone number. Three of them became counseling clients. Later, I totaled up all the money I charged those three clients for psychotherapy sessions, and it came out to about nine hundred dollars. Although getting new business wasn't my intention, I had a new understanding of how tithing can be both spiritually and financially rewarding.

14. *Why do you think tithing has been a recommended practice in so many different religious traditions?*

15. *Why did Paul (of the New Testament) write, "The love of money is the root of all kinds of evil"?*

16. *Why do some people do terrible things to one another, such as rape, murder, and the like?*

17. *Why do bad things sometimes happen to good people?*

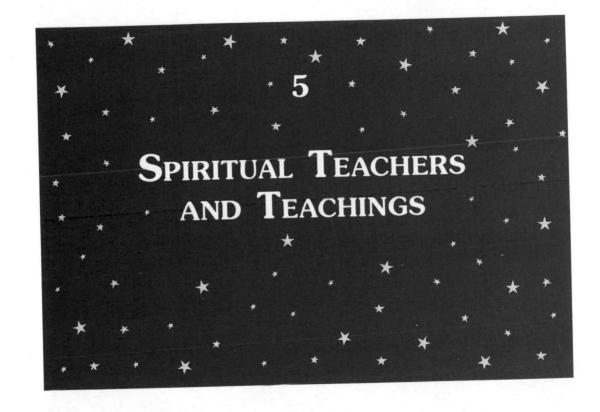

5

SPIRITUAL TEACHERS AND TEACHINGS

To know what we do not know is the beginning of wisdom.
—Indian saying

Buddha, Jesus, Krishna, Mohammed—just mentioning a famous spiritual teacher's name can evoke strong feelings. Since our early childhood, most of us were fed very subjective ideas about spiritual teachers and their teachings. Frequently, we were taught to be suspicious or afraid of teachings that were foreign to us. In extreme cases, fears of other religious teachings have led to prolonged wars. Nowadays, our discomfort with other teachers can keep us from understanding the powerful insights they offer.

In order to love someone, it is not required that we like everything about them. In the same way, in order to gain value from a spiritual teaching, it is not required that we agree with everything it says. Often, lasting impressions are created from hearing bizarre and highly negative stories about a particular religion. By moving past these prejudiced accounts, it's possible to become open to whole new sources of spiritual inspiration and wisdom.

For seven years, I spent many hours per week with a spiritual teacher and the group of students he assisted. He taught me many lessons. One was that growth and joy come from taking on new, seemingly impossible challenges. He tended to give assignments that were in direct opposition to a person's abilities. For example, because I knew nothing about cars, I was put in charge of fixing his car. Since I knew nothing about donkeys, I had to take care of them as we crossed the Sahara Desert on foot. And because I am ignorant when it comes to fashion, I became the fashion coordinator for a major fashion show we produced. When I would tell friends and family about the latest task I was given by my teacher, they would frequently listen with suspicion. I could practically see the word *cult* weaving through their mind. Yet, by the time I completed the unusual tasks I was given, I was stronger—both psychologically and spiritually. Now, when life gives me a seemingly impossible challenge, I complain less. Thanks to my former teacher, I can better see the potential benefit of various life tasks and spiritual teachings.

The questions that follow have two purposes. First, they can help make you aware of any biases you may have concerning various teachers and their teachings. By becoming aware and letting go of old prejudices, you can be more receptive to new sources of inspiration. Second, these questions will assist you in further exploring the wisdom of various spiritual teachings. Enjoy.

1. Do you believe that Jesus Christ was uniquely the "son of God"? If so, what does that mean to you?

2. What do you think of the Pope?

3. Is there anyone alive today whom you consider to be a true spiritual teacher for you? If so, what is it that has persuaded you to accept him or her as a spiritual teacher?

When I was in India, I visited a guru named Sathya Sai Baba. Sai Baba is probably the most respected guru in India, partly because he is known for manifesting things out of thin air. Skeptical of these reports, I went to see for myself. Because I am an amateur magician, I know how someone could use sleight of hand to make small objects "materialize." The first time I saw Sai Baba, I was in a seated crowd of about five thousand people. As he walked through the crowd, he appeared to manifest small amounts of ashes from his fingertips. Unfortunately, I couldn't see well enough to conclude if this was real magic or just a trick.

As I wondered about his abilities, he walked directly over to me and placed his hand about twelve inches from my face. Out of an empty hand, streams of ashes fell onto my lap. I carefully looked for trickery, but found none. After several seconds of this, he looked at me and said, "Satisfied, magic man?" Yes, I was very satisfied.

4. *Do you think spiritual teachers really possess magical powers, such as the ability to walk on water, manifest objects, or heal people? What makes you believe the way you do?*

5. *Of Buddhism, Christianity, Hinduism, Islam, and Judaism, which do you feel the most negative toward? How did that negative impression come about?*

6. *Which religious teacher or teaching do you like the most? What about that teacher or teaching have you found to be particularly helpful?*

7. If you were stranded on a desert island for six months with a spiritual teacher other than the one you mentioned in the previous question, whom would you choose? Why?

8. Of the teachings of Buddha, Jesus, Krishna, and Mohammed, which do you know the least about? Why?

9. Do you believe that teachers who no longer have a body, such as Jesus or the Buddha, are still "alive" in some way? In what way?

10. Do you think it's best to fully dive into a single spiritual teaching, or to explore various paths and learn from each? Why?

11. Can religious teachings become outdated? For example, do you think that everything Jesus, Mohammed, or Moses said still applies today, or is some of it no longer applicable? Why?

When faced with major decisions, I frequently ask God to somehow show me what course I should take. Recently, I had a yearning to go to India, but as a college instructor, the only time I could go would be during the Christmas holidays. My girlfriend didn't like that idea, so I asked God what I should do. My inner guidance said nothing.

That very same night, I was surfing through channels on the TV when I spotted a "preacher" show. In the past, I have avoided such shows because I didn't like how they were always asking for money. Yet, a voice in my head said I should watch this one. The first thing I heard the preacher say was, "You need to go to India. You need to spend a month in India and see how those people live." As my ears perked up, I thought, What an interesting coincidence.

The next line the preacher said practically knocked me off my chair. He looked straight into the camera and said, "Jonathan, you *especially* need to go to India." I have no logical answer as to why he said my name, but that's what I clearly heard. The next day, I bought my tickets.

What questions could you ask God about? If you have a major decision to make or would just like some guidance, give it a try. Then be on the lookout for any strange coincidences that come your way.

12. Imagine that God is here in the room with you in whatever form you most identify with (such as Jesus, if you're a Christian). What one question would you ask God? What do you think God's answer would be? What would you want to say to God?

13. *Do you think all great spiritual teachers have a similar message? If so, what is that message?*

14. *What are a couple of the most powerful teachings you've received from the Bible? If you're familiar with the Bhagavad-Gita, the Koran, or the Buddha's teachings, what are the most powerful teachings you've received from those sources?*

15. *If your favorite spiritual teacher who is no longer living were suddenly alive, what do you think he or she would think of our culture? How do you think his or her teaching would be accepted or changed to fit into today's world?*

6

PEAK EXPERIENCES

I will praise you, O Lord, with all my heart;
I will tell of all your wonders. I will be glad and rejoice in you.
—Psalm 9:1-2

What is a peak experience? There are no simple criteria. It is an extremely personal event that stands out as somehow being more positive, powerful, and important than the normal occurrences of our everyday life. For some people, it could be during the emotional intensity of seeing their baby born; for others, it could be as simple as meditating in a redwood forest. Because peak experiences can affect us so deeply, we often think of them as being "spiritual" (whatever *that* term means). As we think about the peak experiences we've had in the past, we can learn valuable information that can lead to more frequent peak experiences in the future.

When asking people the questions in this chapter, you may find them to be a bit shy in answering at first. For someone to reveal the details of their peak experiences, he or she must feel safe in your presence. Be sure to create an environment that shows you really respect the person you're questioning. Gently inquire for more details if at first they are hesitant to talk about these intimate experiences. As a sense of safety is established, people become more open to sharing such memories.

Discussing our past peak or spiritual experiences can have many valuable effects. When we share such stories, it's easy to become inspired to once again partake of these magical moments. And in this age of violence, cynicism, and distraction, sharing inspirational stories is more important than ever. Without frequent reminders of the beauty that's possible in this world, we can fall victim to the barrage of negativity that surrounds us. Let your reflections on life's greatest moments fill you with new hope and valuable insights.

1. What constitutes a peak experience for you—feelings of deep love, awe, peace, ecstasy, or some other emotion?

2. Do you think peak or spiritual experiences can be brought about by your actions, or are they simply a product of God's grace? Why do you believe the way you do?

3. What do you consider to be the most spiritual experience you have ever had? Please describe it, including what about the experience made it feel "spiritual."

A vision quest is a spiritual adventure, a journey taken in search of something personally meaningful. Many years ago, I arranged to make such a quest to the Anza-Borego Desert. I decided to hitchhike the four-hundred-mile journey, beginning at 4:00 in the morning. Around 7:00 A.M., feeling dejected and cold, and not having gotten a single ride, I walked into a coffee shop, thinking of heading back home. As I stepped through the door, I heard music playing over the sound system. The song was "To Dream the Impossible Dream." I took it as a sign that I should continue my journey. Several times, when I was about to give up, someone would offer me a ride. One elderly man said, "I never pick up hitchhikers, but I felt like God told me to give you a ride."

Finally, I made it to my destination. In the starkness of the beautiful desert, I had the most magical experience of my life. Several hours after my arrival, five balls of light flew toward me from the horizon and danced around me for about three minutes. Intuitively, I knew them to be angels. These beings emanated a joy and playfulness that defies description. My quest for a spiritual adventure had been achieved. In fact, I think anytime we sincerely quest for a deeper connection to Spirit, we are helped. Divine grace awaits our courageous efforts and sincere invitations.

4. *What factors (such as nature, certain people, or techniques) have helped you have peak experiences in the past?*

5. *What are some of the things that seem to cut you off from having profound spiritual experiences more frequently?*

6. *What do you think allows some people to experience peak experiences while others seem to never be so fortunate?*

7. *Is there a special place you can go in which having a highly meaningful experience is almost guaranteed? If so, what makes it so special to you?*

8. Is there a particular person you can go see who is likely to trigger a highly important or meaningful experience for you? If so, what is it about being in his or her presence that seems to affect you?

9. Think back to a couple of your most deeply spiritual experiences. How would you describe what you were feeling and thinking during these moments?

One hot summer day, a friend and I went for a long hike. Somewhere along the way, we lost the trail and couldn't seem to find our way back. It soon became dark and chilly, and we were still lost. Anxiously, I began to force my way through thick brush and branches, desperately hoping to find some sign of civilization. My friend followed closely behind me. By now, I was close to panic, totally irritated, and thoroughly frustrated. I turned to see how my friend was doing, and, with a beaming smile, he said, "Isn't this great? I feel as high as a kite! This is the most fun I've had in years." I was too embarrassed to say how I was reacting to the situation. I quietly kept making my way through the dense brush, now upset that my friend was having a great time while I was freaking out.

Eventually, we rested for the night in the middle of the dense brush. My friend continued to beam delightedly. I continued to be annoyed, anxious, cold, and whiny. In the morning, my friend's good cheer continued undaunted as we once again searched for the trail. Finally, I let go of my upset. I guess I got sick and tired of being sick and tired. We began to sing silly songs as we plowed our way through the brush. By the time we found the trail, we were both feeling an extraordinary sense of adventure. I turned to my friend and said, "How about we do this again sometime?" He smiled.

10. *Have you ever been with someone when they were having a highly spiritual experience? What was that like for you?*

11. *Do you have a spiritual fantasy? That is, do you have an experience you fantasize or think about that motivates you to progress spiritually? If so, what is it?*

12. *Think back to three highly spiritual experiences you've had. Would you say they all felt similar, or was each unique?*

13. Over the past year, what was the most fulfilling moment you can remember? What about it made it so special?

Peak Experience Meditation

In this guided meditation, you'll have an opportunity to relive a past peak experience from your life. Besides the fact that doing such a thing feels good, it can help us learn to access such feelings whenever we want to. With practice, we can open to wonderful and profound feelings quickly and easily.

You may wish to record the following guided meditation with a cassette recorder. This will make it easier for you to relax and vividly remember the details of past precious moments. When recording, read the meditation very slowly, giving yourself plenty of time to fully engage and enjoy the experience. Where you see the word *(pause),* you should be silent for about thirty seconds to allow time to follow the guided meditation instructions. Ideally, this exercise takes about five minutes to complete.

Find a comfortable chair. Take a couple of deep breaths and relax. (If you've already recorded this meditation onto a cassette, you can start the tape now. If not, try to remember the basic outline of this exercise and recall it as best you can.)

Think of one of the most special, wonderful, and intense experiences you have ever had in your life. *(pause for about thirty seconds)* If several of them come to mind, decide to focus on just one of them for now. *(pause)* As you remember this precious experience, allow yourself to recall as many details as you can. *(pause)* Remember exactly where you were and what the weather was like, if you were outdoors. If you were with people, picture what they were doing. *(pause)* Remember the sounds you were hearing and the thoughts you were thinking. Imagine them as if you were experiencing them right now. See if you can recapture what you were feeling. *(pause)* When you get a glimmer of what you were feeling, with each breath allow the feeling to expand throughout your body. *(pause)* If distracting thoughts arise, just let them go as you exhale, and once again breathe in the sense and feeling of your special experience. *(pause)* Whenever you're ready— take as much time as you want—slowly open your eyes and come back to the room you're in.

7

METHODS
OF AWAKENING

Feeling is God's mirror; intuition is God's telephone.
—Kenny Loggins

In my book *Bridges to Heaven,* I asked thirty-eight well-known spiritual seekers ten questions about how they deepen their connection with God. I was surprised to find the incredible range of answers I received. Indeed, I could not tell the contributors' religious persuasion by the ways they deepened their contact with God. For example, some Christian contributors used the same methods as some Buddhists. With the great variety of responses I received, I realized that no matter what their religious persuasion, each person had unique and highly individualized ways of seeking the divine.

As a psychotherapist, I often notice how couples get into ruts in how they spend their intimate time together. In our relationship to Spirit, there is also a tendency to get mired in routines that no longer bring us the divine intimacy they once did. Unfortunately, people can get "religious" about the "right" way to grow spiritually, and thereby overlook other beneficial methods. When this occurs, what can result is a lack of direct spiritual experience. By taking an inventory of how well specific spiritual practices have worked in the past, and which methods we've overlooked, we are better able to ascertain promising areas for future spiritual exploration.

Spiritual techniques can be grouped into three categories: those that primarily work on the mind (such as meditation), those that work on the body (such as yoga), and those that work by opening the heart (such as prayer). Although any of these methods can lead to divine intimacy, it can be interesting to focus on those that are different from what we're accustomed to. The questions that follow can help make you aware of new ways to connect with your spiritual essence.

1. What is your favorite way to connect with a sense of the divine? For example, do you connect with the divine through time in nature, church, meditation?

2. Do you believe that someone can grow spiritually through the use of psychedelic drugs such as LSD? Why or why not?

3. If you pray, do you always pray the same way or do you sometimes try something new? What exactly do you do when you pray?

4. If you meditate, what have you found to be your most satisfying form of meditation?

Years ago, I read a book called *Lucid Dreaming*. It details several ways to become aware that you're dreaming *while* you're dreaming. The first time I experienced this was especially humorous. In a dream, I had learned how to fly without the aid of an airplane. I was busy showing off my miraculous abilities to anyone who would watch. While flying through the air, a friend of mine on the ground explained to me that I was "only dreaming." I defensively told her she was mistaken, that I really could fly. She insisted otherwise, and we got into an argument over whether I was dreaming or not. Through her clever cross-examination, her reasoning prevailed. I was disappointed and sank to earth. But, realizing that I could do whatever I wanted since this was a dream, I began to soar again. Now, when I realize I'm dreaming, I try to take full advantage of it. I'll frequently imagine I'm sitting before "God," free to ask Him any question. So far, He hasn't given me the right numbers to win the lottery, but His other advice has been very helpful!

5. *Do you think working with your dreams can help you grow spiritually? Why?*

6. *What helps you differentiate the chatter of your mind from true divine or intuitive guidance?*

7. *What has been frustrating for you about contacting God?*

8. *Do you ever try to contemplate an idea or a quote from a holy book as a way of deepening your spiritual connection? If so, what is that like for you?*

I was at Mammoth ski resort with a couple of friends when we came upon a huge rock used for rock climbing. Having climbed with ropes once before, I was eager to try my luck. I had someone hold my rope in case I fell, and I eagerly launched myself at the rock. Unknowingly, I had chosen the hardest part of the rock to climb, the side reserved for only the most advanced climbers. As I climbed the rock, everything seemed to just "click" for me. I'd leap for a handhold I couldn't even see, and somehow I'd get it. Instead of feeling afraid of falling, I confidently made it to the top. It was a feeling of great exhilaration. Later, I learned that even many advanced climbers can't make it up that side of the rock. To impress my friends, later that day I tried again but couldn't even make it three feet off the ground. It was then I realized that getting to the top of that rock had taken resources and faith beyond what I normally possess. It had been a spiritual experience.

9. *Do you ever use techniques that are body oriented, such as yoga, tai chi chuan, rock climbing, breathing exercises, or intensive dance, as a way of connecting with your divine essence? If so, what has worked best for you?*

10. *What method have you rarely or never used but which has struck you as a potentially helpful way of deepening your spiritual connection?*

11. What method are you currently using that no longer seems to be very inspiring or useful in your spiritual growth?

12. Is there any group or organization that you think could help you along your spiritual path? If you're not part of this group now, what keeps you from becoming involved?

13. What activities most help you to quiet your mind and/or open your heart?

14. Of the following list of spiritual methods, which ones haven't you tried? Why? Do any call to you now?

    a. prayer
    b. meditation
    c. hatha yoga
    d. singing devotional songs
    e. contacting spirit guides or angels
    f. building an altar
    g. witnessing your thoughts or actions in a nonjudgmental manner
       (mindfulness training)

h. *whirling (as with whirling dervishes)*
i. *contemplation and reflection*
j. *prolonged fasting*
k. *celibacy*
l. *prolonged solitude*
m. *pranayama (breathing exercises)*

15. What did you do as a child that made you feel safe and content inside? Might this be something you could do today for the same effect?

I was worried about my brother. He had seemed pretty down for quite a while. As the family counselor, it was my duty to talk to him. When he expressed that he didn't know what he wanted to do with his life, I asked him, "If you had six months left to live, what would you do? Would you still do what you're doing?"

Without hesitation, he responded, "The only question is whether I would bother taking twenty seconds to call my boss to tell him I quit my job. Then, I'd travel around the world."

To make a long story short, soon thereafter he quit his job and traveled around the world. Now he's back home, doing more of what he really wants to do. Each time I see him, he looks happier and happier.

16. If you had six months left to live, what would you do with your time? Are you doing many (or any) of those things in your current life?

8

MIRACLES AND THEIR MEANINGS

Just behind the visible world is a whole other world in which it all works differently.
—Ram Dass

Have you ever witnessed or taken part in what you considered to be a "miracle"? Most people have. Be they psychic phenomena, spontaneous healings, or encounters with spiritual beings, miracles can profoundly affect the way we view ourselves and our world. Although most people have been privy to a miracle sometime in their life, such experiences are rarely shared. We're afraid of looking weird or having an experience we consider sacred be ridiculed by others.

A couple of years ago, I decided to try something new at a party I was hosting with a bunch of friends. I asked everyone at the party to talk about the most miraculous thing they had ever experienced. One by one, people shared stories filled with mystery and magic. Listening to them created an atmosphere of wonderment and reverence. By the end of the evening, we shared a bond that came from recognizing the magical nature of the world we live in.

Perhaps the strangest workshop I've ever taken was a course in "spoon bending." In this seminar, you learn how to bend spoons with the power of your mind. The instructor gives everyone a spoon and then explains, "To bend a spoon, you must *demand* that it bend. *Scream* at your spoon to bend. Yell at it with all the power in your soul. Then, just forget about it. Start a conversation with your neighbor, think of something else, just forget about the spoon." Like a bunch of complete lunatics, we all began yelling at our spoons to bend. After yelling for a couple of minutes at our spoons, we started laughing. While we were doubling over in laughter at the craziness of what we were doing, our spoons began doubling over, too. They actually bent before our eyes!

I have witnessed many miracles, but this one affected me in a unique way. It helped me clearly see that our thoughts really impact the material world. Now when I pray, I do it with a bit more faith and certainty (the yelling is optional). Then I let go and wait for the magic.

When we reflect on miracles we've experienced, or listen to the miraculous stories of our friends, we can easily tap into a sense of wonder. In the questions that follow, you will have an opportunity to examine your beliefs about miracles and perhaps how you limit them in your life. More important, you'll have the chance to remember and reexperience the wonder of living in a mysterious universe.

1. What is the most miraculous thing you've ever experienced or witnessed?

2. Have you ever experienced something that could be considered a psychic event? What happened?

3. What is the difference between a psychic experience (or correct intuition) and a miracle?

4. What are the signals of your intuition? Do you see pictures in your mind, hear an intuitive voice, perceive a certain feeling?

5. When you've experienced or witnessed a miracle, how has it affected your view of "reality"?

6. Do you think that Jesus really walked on water and healed the sick as reported in the Bible? Why?

One day, my sister asked me to baby-sit my four-year-old nephew for a few hours. As an amateur magician, I thought it would be fun to teach him some simple magic tricks. He was awed and excited by the magic, but once I showed him how I did the tricks, he quickly lost interest.

As the day progressed, I noticed that my nephew kept asking me the question: Why? He'd say, "Why is the sky blue?" or, "Why are trees green?" At first, I would try to answer his questions. But each time I did, his childlike wonder seemed diminished. I realized that adults are the same way. Once we know (or think we know) how something works, we lose our ability to be in wonder and awe. Finally, each time he'd ask a "Why" question, I refused to squelch his curiosity. I'd simply say, "I don't know; I guess it must be pure magic." He always liked that answer.

7. What is your explanation for how miracles and/or psychic phenomena occur? What, if anything, determines when they happen?

8. Do you believe that prayer can change the outcome of events? Why?

9. Do you believe in the miracles of the Old Testament, such as when the Red Sea parted? Why?

10. Have you shared stories with friends and family of miracles you've experienced? If so, what was that like for you? What were their reactions?

11. Do you think science will someday have an explanation for such things as psychic phenomena and spontaneous healings, or will they always be a mystery?

I have participated in many "fire walk workshops." In these gatherings, people walk barefoot over eighteen-hundred-degree coals, hopefully without getting burned. The technique used in this seemingly impossible feat (pun intended) is very simple: The fire walk leader suggests standing in front of the coals and "asking God or your Higher Self if it's safe for you to walk across the coals. Then notice how your body feels. If it's safe, you'll feel an opening and relaxation in your body. Then you can walk. If it's not safe, you'll feel a closing down or contraction in your body."

In the fourth fire walk I participated in, I was beginning to feel that walking over burning coals was no big deal. In my first three attempts, I was never burned, so I thought asking for divine guidance was not really necessary. So on my fourth attempt, I didn't bother asking if it was safe to cross the coals, and confidently walked across. About halfway across the coals, I had a rather rude awakening. The coals seemed *extremely* hot! My feet soon had blisters all over them. Humbled, I now know that asking for guidance from within can yield miraculous results. The next time you're standing in front of burning coals (or a situation that feels like it), and you're wondering what to do, ask within if it's safe to proceed. Your feet will thank me for it.

12. What, if anything, can you do to increase the likelihood of something miraculous occurring? For example, do you think that prayer, a particular attitude, a special place, or being with certain people can help?

13. Do you believe angels or spirit guides can help people when they are in trouble? Why?

14. Do you believe it's possible to learn how to have miraculous powers (such as the ability to heal or to know the future), or are such things always a "gift"?

15. If you assume that miracles (such as spontaneous healings and psychic phenomena) actually take place, why do they happen to some people and not others?

9

DEATH AND BEYOND

Life is a great mystery; then you become one.
—Russ Rogers

Death is not a welcomed subject in this culture. You almost never hear people bring it up in conversation—even in hospitals. Perhaps we think if we don't talk about it, it'll go away. This avoidance of death is a cultural phenomenon. People in many other cultures talk openly about death—and even celebrate its arrival. Since our beliefs about death and reactions to it are largely influenced by our society, it's important we reexamine what we really *do* believe. By looking at our deepest beliefs about death, the way we live our lives can be altered.

In workshops I lead about spiritual growth, I often have participants contemplate their own death and evaluate what they want to accomplish by the time they die. Carlos Castenada's teacher, Don Juan, used to tell Carlos to "use death as an advisor." Somehow, the knowledge of our impending death puts our daily upsets and struggles into perspective and can compel us to stop putting off our deepest desires.

People who have had close brushes with death will often reevaluate the course of their lives and make changes based on their profound experience. However, it's not necessary to have a near-death experience in order to use death as an adviser. Death is always nearby, willing to remind us that life is short. Planet Earth is like an airport for souls, with thousands of arrivals and departures each hour. The questions that follow can serve to remind us what's truly important during our brief sojourn here—and help us get back on track if we've strayed off course.

1. Have you ever had a close brush with death? If so, what happened and what was that like for you?

2. Do you believe people go to heaven or hell after they die? If so, what do you think heaven and hell are like?

3. Many people who have had a near-death experience report that, during their life review, they are asked a question by "God" or the "Being of Light" they meet. Regardless of culture or religious beliefs, the question they are reportedly asked is very much the same. Some people who have had this experience say that it's as if our whole life is a test to learn the answer to this one question: What have you learned about being able to love?

4. If you knew beyond any doubt that how you live on Earth affects what happens to you when you die, would you live any differently? If so, how?

5. What do you think of the stories of people who have been clinically dead for a short time and come back to report profound encounters with dead loved ones, Beings of Light, and the like?

In the days of the Buddha, it is said there was a brutal murderer who used to go to the monasteries and kill the monks. Whenever the monks heard that this man was near, they would flee to the hills. One day, the murderer heard there was a single monk who decided not to flee the monastery. This enraged the murderer. He swaggered into the monastery, walked up to the monk, and boasted, "Don't you know who I am? I could take my sword and run it through your belly without batting an eye!"

The monk looked up at the fierce man before him and gently asked him, "And don't you know who I am? I could have your sword run right through my belly—without batting an eye."

According to the legend, the murderer gave up his violent ways and became a monk.

6. *What about death do you find scary or particularly disturbing? Is there anything you could do to lessen your fear?*

7. *Have you ever seen or felt the presence of someone who is dead? If so, what happened?*

8. *How would you like to die? Why?*

9. How old would you like to be when you die? Why?

10. If you died tomorrow, what would you regret not having done?

11. If you died tomorrow, what do you think people would say about you at your funeral? What would you like them to say?

12. Do you believe in reincarnation? Why?

13. Why do we hide from the reality of death in this culture?

14. Would you like to be buried or cremated? Why?

One day while reading his morning paper, Alfred Nobel came upon a very disturbing article. To his surprise, he was reading his own obituary! What's more, the obituary reported that Mr. Nobel was responsible for creating a new, more powerful form of dynamite. It went on to say how this new form of dynamite had maimed and killed countless people, and that Mr. Nobel had become a rich man because of it. In that moment, Alfred Nobel vowed to be known for something other than killing people by the time his time was truly up.

He asked himself, What would I like to be remembered for? He decided he wanted to be known for great contributions to humanity. He instituted the Nobel Prize for great advancements in the areas of peace, chemistry, literature, physics, and medicine. Ironically, he financed the prize through the money he made from selling dynamite. Nowadays, he's remembered for establishing the coveted awards, which encourage and celebrate the finest human achievements.

15. After you're dead, for what do you want to be remembered?

16. How do you feel about donating your organs, such as your heart or eyes, in the event of an accidental death? Have you made your wishes known in your will?

17. If you've made out a will, what was that process like for you? If you haven't made out a will, why not?

Meditation on Death and Dying

It's very hard to imagine our own death. It's as if we have a wall in our brain that makes it difficult to even *think* of such a thing. Yet, the reality is we will someday die. By piercing through our denial of death, it's possible to live our life with more gratitude for the precious gift of life we've been given.

In order to fully experience each part of this meditation, it can be helpful to record this exercise. Whether speaking into a tape recorder, having a friend read it to you, or remembering it on your own, take your time with each section.

Sit in a comfortable chair and take a couple of slow, deep breaths. Begin thinking of a time you found out that someone you knew quite well had died. Try to remember what your reaction was. Was it surprise? Shock? Sadness? *(pause)* Remember what it felt like to realize that you could never see this person again. *(pause)* Now, think of an acquaintance you work with. Randomly choose one person. Imagine them getting older and more frail. Imagine them on their deathbed, gasping for air. *(pause)* Imagine them taking their last breath and dying. *(pause)* Now, imagine someone you care deeply about. Imagine them getting older and more frail. *(pause)* Imagine them on their deathbed, gasping for air. Imagine them taking their last breath and dying. *(pause)* Realize that everyone you've ever known—your parents, your friends, your coworkers—will someday be gone. *(pause)* Now, imagine yourself getting older and becoming more frail. Imagine yourself on your deathbed, gasping for air. *(pause)* Imagine looking back on your life and reflecting on what you did and did not do. *(pause)* From this vantage point, ask yourself: Have I lived the way I truly wanted to live? *(pause)* Is there anything I wish I had done that I never did? *(pause)* Imagine taking your last breath and dying.

10

THE FUTURE OF SPIRIT

The soul force is indestructible and it goes on gaining power
until it transforms everyone it touches.
—Mohandas K. Gandhi

Technology has had a profound impact on most areas of our lives, and spirituality is no exception. At one time, spiritual matters were handled by a chosen class of people, such as priests and Brahmans. With the decentralization of power that technology brings, we now have much greater authority over our spiritual destiny. What will we do with this freedom?

Besides giving us more choices over our destiny, technology also burdens us with new ethical and moral questions. As science shows us how to manipulate our genes, our brains, and perhaps even our souls, we will face profound spiritual questions about our role in the universe. In addition, we will have to decide if the "mind machines" of tomorrow can be a useful aid to spiritual development.

As a psychotherapist, I've seen that telling people they need to change does not work. When couples come to me for counseling, each partner frequently hopes I'll talk to the other about how wrong he or she has been, and how that partner needs to change. Instead, I ask questions that get each person to see the likely future outcome of continuing the current behavior. For example, recently a couple I'll call Bob and Sue came to me because, according to Sue, Bob watched too much TV. Sue lectured Bob about how he was ruining their marriage. As Sue talked, I watched Bob gradually become more defensive and withdrawn from his wife.

When it was my turn to speak, I asked each a question to help them reevaluate their behavior. To Sue I asked, "What makes you think Bob is going to change when you lecture him, since every time you've lectured him in the past he's just become more obstinate and withdrawn?" Sue finally got it—nagging only made the situation worse. To Bob I asked, "What is likely to happen if you continue to watch TV and not do the things that help your wife feel more loved?"

Bob responded, "I guess we would end up divorced." When he concluded that he didn't want a divorce, he became more receptive to change. A thought-provoking question has more power to change someone's behavior than even the most persuasive lecture.

In the questions that follow, you'll have an opportunity to reflect on many possible scenarios. You'll be asked to imagine how things are likely to change for you and humanity in the coming years. By projecting ourselves into the future, we can sometimes avoid pitfalls that lie directly in our path. You'll also be guided to reflect on how the factors of age, money, and changing life circumstances can affect your spiritual destiny.

1. If you consistently follow your deepest spiritual longings, how do you think you'll be different in ten years? If you fail to follow your heart over this period of time, how do you think you'd be different?

2. Do you foresee a spiritual renaissance in this society in the next decade? If so, where do you think it will lead? What do you foresee happening to the spiritual condition and beliefs of humanity over the next hundred years?

3. What do you think will most help or hinder the human race toward a greater spiritual awakening in the coming age?

When I was in my early twenties, I spent a couple of hours each week volunteering at a retirement home. My spiritual teacher at the time required that I do volunteer work in order to have access to his teachings. Initially, I hated going. The place smelled bad; many of the people were senile, sick, or in pain; and I didn't know what to say to them. Although they appreciated someone coming to talk to them, I also sensed that they felt uncomfortable being a "charity case." Then, I met Vye. Vye was eighty-nine years young, blind as a bat, full of life and laughter, and always an adventure to be with. One day, her sparkling personality moved me to ask, "What advice can you give a young person like me about how to live a successful life?"

What she said both touched me and made me laugh: "Don't take life so seriously. After all, it's not permanent."

From that day onward, I asked each elderly person at the retirement home the same question. Seeking their advice on how to live a successful life would always engage their interest and allow them to espouse their heartfelt philosophy. I began to enjoy my weekly visits. I started feeling like *I* was the "charity case" and that they were helping *me* through sharing their accumulated life wisdom. After a few months of visits, I was informed that Vye had passed away. I remember how sad I felt; I remember that a tear rolled down my face. But with that tear, I could hear her gentle voice saying, "Don't take life so seriously. After all, it's not permanent." From time to time, her words still guide me back from the depths of seriousness to the shores of serenity.

4. Imagine yourself in the future, sitting in your rocking chair. As an old and wise person, what advice would you give to the person you are today?

5. Over the past hundred years, do you think humanity as a whole has grown spiritually? Why?

6. Do you think that technological devices, such as flashing "sound and light" machines now being sold, can help people to have spiritual experiences and grow spiritually? Why?

7. If there were a totally safe pill you could take or machine you could use to induce profound spiritual experiences, would you use it? Why? What effect do you think such inventions would have on humanity?

8. What effect do you think growing older will have on your spiritual practice? What different spiritual needs do you anticipate?

In the Bible, it says, "Ask and ye shall receive." As a spiritual experiment many years ago, I went on a six-week hitchhiking trip across the United States. I deliberately took no money. Instead of paying for food or shelter, I decided I would simply ask people for whatever I needed. As I got ready for the trip, I occasionally told people about my plans. Almost without exception, friends and family would look at me as if I had just lost my marbles and say, "You can't do that. You'll be dead within a week." I started to doubt myself, but my intuition said I'd be taken care of.

Once on the trip, it became routine to go to markets and ask for food, or to knock on people's doors and ask if I could sleep in their house or yard. When I tell this story in seminars I lead, people usually assume that I was rejected a lot. In fact, more than 90 percent of the people I approached offered me food or shelter. When we make ourselves vulnerable and ask directly for help, the generosity inside people is often called forth. "Ask and ye shall receive." Good advice, even after 2,000 years.

9. *How do you think a major change in your financial situation (for the better or the worse) would change your spiritual life? Do you think having a lot of money or being totally broke would affect your spiritual pursuits in a positive way?*

10. *Do you have a plan to enhance your spiritual experience of life with the money you now have or the money you hope to make in the future? If so, what's your*

plan? If you don't have a plan, consider how you might use an extra ten thousand dollars to enhance the level of peace and love you have in your life.

11. How do you think getting married (or divorced), or having kids (or not having kids), will affect your personal spiritual development?

12. Who do you think should be given the moral authority to determine if a person can end his or her own life? Who should determine how many kids you can have in an overpopulated, overpolluted world? How should decisions about the legality of manipulating human genes or cloning people be made?

13. How do you think religion, spirituality, and politics will influence one another over the coming decades?

11

MOVING
BEYOND THE MIND

Freedom is emptying the mind of experience.
—J. Krishnamurti

In the Zen Buddhist tradition, there is a technique for experiencing enlightenment, called "koan study." A koan is a question the Zen master gives a student to contemplate during times of meditation. These questions have no logical or rational answer. The most well-known koan is the question: What is the sound of one hand clapping? By intensely contemplating such riddles, a Zen student can sometimes go beyond intellectual reasoning and have a direct and profound experience of ultimate reality.

As a child, I remember sometimes contemplating such unanswerable questions. My favorite mind-blowing question was: What's at the end of the universe?

I would repeatedly try to picture an end to the universe, but, of course, there was always boundless space after my imagined end. The realization and, occasionally, the *experience* that the universe can have no end led to a direct experience of the concept of infinity. It was very exhilarating.

As times and cultures change, a need arises for appropriate new koans. In fact, the science of quantum physics has handed us several seemingly impossible paradoxes about the ultimate nature of reality. These riddles of nature are simply more evidence that the great mysteries of life cannot be fully comprehended with the rational, thinking mind. As Albert Einstein said, "The truly important thing is intuition."

The questions that follow have no logical answer. Think of them as a launching pad for expanding the limits of the rational mind—and perhaps leaping off into the great unknown. I have found that pondering these unanswerable questions often leads to deep frustration and confusion. Such feelings mean you're probably making progress. Keep plowing forward, repeating the question to yourself as your mind tries to avoid its possible demise. Eventually, the linear mind burns itself out, and what remains is very profound.

After each question, I clarify the implicit paradox or provide a hint as to how to approach it. A paradox is simply how multidimensional reality looks to our dualistic thinking mind. By diving into these paradoxes and puzzles, see if you can experience a moment of "satori"—a sudden intuitive realization of the nature of reality.

1. How can a particle exist that has no mass? (According to quantum mechanics, such particles do exist. Trying to imagine such a thing can definitely stretch the mind.)

2. Who were you before you were born? (Imagine going back before you were born and sensing who/what you were.)

3. What would it be like if you never were born? (Imagine never existing for all of eternity. If you begin to feel fear, you're probably on the right track.)

4. What is infinity? (When human beings try to "grasp" infinity, it provides endless amusement for God.)

5. *What lies at the end of infinity? How does infinity end? (Picture a far-off edge to the universe, with a wall at the end. Then realize that on the other side of the wall, the universe still goes on forever. Keep repeating this image until smoke comes out of your ears and your mind shuts down.)*

6. *How did God come into being? Or, if you don't believe in God, How did the universe come into being? (If you keep going back to how anything ever got here, you see that somewhere, somehow, something far beyond logic had to have happened. Dive into that mystery and enjoy swimming around.)*

7. *What existed before God? Or, what existed before the universe came into being? (Try to imagine total, absolute nothingness. Even empty space implies an "other" that is not empty.)*

It is said that someone once asked the Buddha how long our souls have been going through the cycles of death and rebirth. The Buddha is reported to have said, "Imagine a mountain the size of Everest. Imagine that once every one hundred years, a bird could fly over this mountain with a silk in its beak. Imagine that this silk would ever so gently skim the very top of this mountain as the bird flew over it. The length of time it would take for that silk to erode the mountain down to nothing is the length of time your essence has been in existence."

8. *What is eternity? When will eternity end? (Imagine the longest length of time possible. Then, imagine a "forever" beyond that, and beyond that, and beyond that . . .)*

9. *When you think to move your arm, how do you do it? (When you look at anything in enough microscopic detail, you begin to realize that we really don't know how anything works. It's all magic.)*

10. *From what source do your thoughts arise? (Try following each thought back to where it originated. A mystery and/or void awaits you.)*

11. *If the universe is truly infinite, does that mean in some galaxy there is some other person with your name and looks, acting just like you? (A personal version of the question: If you put enough monkeys in a room with typewriters for a long enough time, would the plays of Shakespeare finally appear?)*

12

INSPIRATION AND SUPPORT

Where there is no vision, people perish.
—Proverbs

Part I ★ Inspiration

This chapter is divided into two parts. In the first part, the questions are designed for finding new sources of inspiration. In part II, the questions are devised to help a friend or family member be accountable to their spiritual aspirations. Inspiration and spiritual support function concurrently, like a gas tank and an engine. Together, they provide the fuel for spiritual effort, along with the power to overcome the obstacles that get in the way. Without inspiration, we can forget why we're making efforts in the first place. Without spiritual accountability and support, our efforts can easily get off track or slowly fade.

In this day and age, we are overwhelmed with disheartening news as the media bombards us with violence and suffering. After a while, it's tempting to just give up hope and become numb. Fortunately, we all have the ability to *decide* what we will allow to enter the doorway of our mind. We can choose to focus on the suffering—or on the solutions. We can choose to watch programs filled with agitation or ones filled with illumination. By surrounding ourselves with information that inspires us, we become more motivated to pursue our deepest dreams.

The questions in part I are most effective if explored with several people. The greater the number of uplifting books, movies and shows we are exposed to, the more we can surround ourselves with a strong sense of hope. Now that we can rent videos, we have access to thousands of uplifting movies. Sometimes I've watched movies ten or more times, because their effect on me is so profound. The same is true for some of my favorite books. They've become like old friends I can always rely on to inspire me when I've lost my way.

The answers to the following questions can provide you with an abundance of uplifting stories and spiritual inspiration.

1. Are there places you go, such as in nature, that revitalize you? Where are some of those places?

2. Is there a church or synagogue you've attended that has been especially spirited or powerful for you?

Wherever I go, there's a question I ask people that immediately leads to an intimate and friendly conversation. This question works just as well for complete strangers as it does for family members. I can even be in a bank line and casually begin a conversation like this: "I'm planning to rent a video tonight, and I don't know what to rent. *I'm wondering, could you recommend a movie that really touched you in a special way?*"

Almost everyone loves to answer this question. It gives people an opportunity to be helpful, which makes them feel good. It also allows them to reminisce about one of their favorite movies. An added bonus about this question is that it gives you immediate insight into the type of person you're dealing with. If the person you're talking to says their favorite movie is *The Texas Chainsaw Massacre,* you quickly thank them—and run away. But if they suggest a more spiritually uplifting movie, you can comfortably begin talking about the types of movies that deeply affect you, and why. I've met many a friend in this manner.

3. What would you say is the most inspiring movie you have ever seen? Why did you like it so much? (See "Resources for Further Exploration" at the back of this book for a list of the twenty most inspiring movies people have reported to me.)

4. What other movies have you found to touch you deeply in a positive way?

5. What nonfiction, self-help book(s) have you found to be of profound help to you? (See "Resources for Further Exploration" at the back of this book for a list of the twenty most inspiring self-help books people have reported to me.)

6. What book(s) of fiction have had an uplifting and positive effect on you?

7. What TV program(s) or plays have you found to be heartwarming and inspiring? Why?

I had enrolled in an expensive weekend acting workshop. The instructor was incredibly boring, and I was beginning to get very aggravated. After twelve hours of telling her life story, the instructor finally gave us something to do: "I want you to pretend you're someone you fully admire, and I want this person to be someone who feels totally different than you feel right now."

At the time, my anger at the instructor made me feel a lot like Charles Manson, so I thought a good contrast would be Saint Francis. The instructions were for us to "become" the person we admire and to go around the room, introducing ourselves as that person. I had always liked Saint Francis' humility and gentleness, and tried to become like him as I chatted with other people in the workshop. Before I knew it, I felt great joy and love for everyone in the room. Because I was overflowing with love, several people began waiting in line to "meet" Saint Francis. Through this experience, Saint Francis became a very alive and important role model for me. Even when I am feeling my worst, I know that the love of Saint Francis (which is within me) is never far away.

8. Who is a spiritual role model that inspires you? What about this person do you aspire to? Try pretending you are that person, or pretend that you fully possess the trait you most admire about that person.

9. What music most uplifts you? Can you name specific musicians or songs that have especially touched you?

10. What poetry or poet have you found to affect you deeply?

11. What artists, art galleries, or piece of artwork has especially moved you?

Part II ★ Spiritual Support

Many people know what they *should* do in order to grow spiritually, but few people follow through. We get lost in the details of life and forget to make time for nurturing our soul. And in a culture that often ridicules spiritual pursuits, it's hard to get the support needed to maintain a spiritual practice. Frequently, even church or synagogue groups can fail to give us spiritual support—especially if they focus too much on social activities.

In most important areas of our life, other people check up after us: We're accountable to our boss or our bottom line at work; in our relationships, we are always accountable for our actions. But, for better or worse, spiritual pursuits are considered a very private matter. It's rare for anyone to ask us how our spiritual practice is going. The result is a tendency to become less disciplined in our spiritual path than in other areas of life.

When we permit someone to ask us questions about our spiritual practice, it allows us to reflect anew on how things are going. We become more disciplined if we know that we have to answer for our actions. By asking important questions, an "accountability partner" can help remind us to stay true to our spiritual path.

For many years, I've met with a friend once a week to go over questions such as the ones that follow. One of us asks a question, and the other just listens, avoiding giving advice. Then we trade roles. The whole meeting takes only about thirty minutes, but it has a tremendous impact on our lives. It helps me quickly notice when I've steered off course and gives me the motivation and awareness to stay consistently true to my deepest aspirations. Perhaps you will want to try using the following questions with a friend. If it works for you, feel free to make up your own "coaching questions," and do it as often as you see fit.

1. What are your deepest aspirations?

2. What was your past week (or month) like? How did you do in staying true to your deepest spiritual aspirations?

3. What did you do this past week that was beneficial to your spiritual growth?

Sometimes, a single question can cut through our illusions and suddenly show us that our whole life is off track. Years ago, I had a patient named Fred who was a workaholic. He had been working fourteen hours a day, seven days a week, for the past five years. He reported that he disliked his job and often complained about it. Because I couldn't understand why he worked so hard, I asked him, "Why are you putting in so much time at work?"

He quickly replied, "So I can finally take some time off and relax." As soon as he said that, the light bulb in his head went off. He realized that his ultimate goal was relaxation and that overworking was moving him in the wrong direction. The next time I saw him, he looked tan and refreshed from a two-week stay in Hawaii.

4. *What would you like your next week to be like?*

5. *What did you do this past week that interfered with your experiencing a deeper spiritual connection?*

6. *Is there any spiritual discipline (such as prayer, yoga, meditation) that you*

would be willing to commit to doing this week? If so, tell me what you're willing to commit to and how often I should check with you to see how you're doing.

7. What one or two small actions could you do this week to nurture your spirit and make your life more peaceful?

There have been times when an unexpected question has prevented me from doing something really stupid. I remember a time when my girlfriend and I were on a much-needed vacation. As we were driving through the city, we were both in a rotten mood and began snapping at each other. Finally, she said something that I felt to be totally untrue, and I decided, in no uncertain terms, to tell her how wrong she was. Just then, I noticed the bumper sticker on the car in front of me: "Are we having fun yet?" The question totally interrupted my ability to launch into my self-righteous tirade. Instead, I took a deep breath, smiled, and sheepishly said, "Are we having fun yet?" She laughed, and we both felt better.

8. If you veer off from where you'd like to be, what can you do to quickly get back on track?

9. What reminders do you have or could you create for yourself for remembering your purpose during this next week?

10. At this point in your life, on a scale of 1 to 10 (with 1 equaling "not at all" and 10 meaning "as good as possible"), how much are you in touch with:

   a. your own heart
   b. divine love
   c. loving others
   d. inner peace
   e. a sense of awe and wonder
   f. service to God/humanity
   g. divine will for you
   h. enjoying life

11. Based on your answers to the preceding question, is there any activity that might be good for you to do in order to be better in balance?

13

LIVING FROM THE HEART

*If you could only love enough, you could be
the most powerful person in the world.*
—Emmet Fox

Part I ★ Mini-meditations

This chapter has two parts. In part I, the questions are designed to be an entrance to a meditative experience. We can give ourselves a wonderful gift by taking time out of our busy schedules to fully engage our higher nature. For those times when we can't disengage from what we're doing, the questions in part II can still help us see things from a more lofty perspective.

When we think of a person who is spiritually evolved, we normally envision someone who is very peaceful, loving, and compassionate. Although there are many religions and methods to help people become "more spiritual," one of the simplest ways to raise our consciousness is through the effective use of questions. By meditating on the following questions, it's possible to experience deep feelings of love, gratitude, tranquillity, and even compassion.

For the questions in this section, the answers are not the important thing. Rather, think of these questions as an opportunity to contemplate a particular *experience*. Like tuning in to a station on the radio, it's possible to tune in to feelings of love and peace through these "mini-meditations." In order to fully immerse yourself in these meditations, allow several minutes for each question. With practice, you can get even better at opening up to the kingdom of heaven within.

When I first began to meditate with the questions in this section, my answers came mostly from my intellect. Yet over time, my intellect learned to relax and allow my heart to receive the answers, usually in the form of highly enjoyable feelings. I have also found that I can deepen the experience by imagining my heart to have lungs. As I breathe slowly and deeply "into my heart," I become more immersed in the feelings of love, gratitude, and peace. Perhaps you will find the same methods to be useful.

1. Who is someone you deeply love or have deeply loved in the past? Picture them in your mind and allow yourself to feel your heartfelt connection with them.

2. When in your life have you felt the most loved? Take some time to remember the many details of what that was like. Who were you with? What were you doing? What allowed you to open to such deep feelings of love? Later, be sure to tell your partner what makes you feel most loved.

3. When in your life have you felt the most loving? Reflect on who you were with and what you were doing at that moment. Allow yourself to reexperience those feelings.

In 1992, I got a ride in a van that delivers people to the local airport. On the way, we hit a patch of ice at sixty miles per hour, and the van overturned several times before skidding to a halt. There were no seat belts, so everyone inside was violently thrown around the van or through the windows. I landed inside the van with the front seat pinning me down. Someone yelled, "Get out of the van, it might explode!" I remember thinking, I wonder if I'm paralyzed? I wonder if I can move my arms? When I managed to get the front seat off my body, I felt overwhelming gratitude for the use of my arms. When I realized that I was able to run out of the van, I felt deep thankfulness for being given the gift of healthy legs. Several people in the van weren't so fortunate.

Now, I always take a few minutes each day to ponder how fortunate I am. If I'm not feeling particularly grateful for how things are going during my day, I'll simply look at my healthy arms and legs. It never fails to bring me a sense of perspective and gratitude.

4. What could you feel grateful for? If you prefer, you can think of several people in your life you feel grateful for. Once you're in touch with a sense of gratitude, allow yourself to be engulfed by the feeling.

5. When in your life have you felt the most peaceful? Reflect on the scene you were in and how your mind and body felt.

6. What do you really appreciate or love about yourself? Even if it's something small, take some time to really feel appreciation and care for yourself.

7. Think of someone you love. Ask yourself, What is it about them that's so lovable? As you think of their positive traits, allow yourself to feel your love and appreciation of them.

8. Where do you feel tense in your body? See if you can fully release all the tension there.

9. What would it be like to spend a couple of days in your favorite relaxing nature spot? Imagine as many details as you can of such an experience and follow the feeling.

10. Have you done anything today to take you away from the experience of love or the experience of God? Open to receive loving feedback on where you may have veered off course. Listen to the still, small voice within.

A couple of years ago, my girlfriend and I were camping out in the middle of the Mojave Desert. I was having a hard time relaxing, because I hadn't yet found a publisher for the book I had been working on for almost two years. I knew

I should simply surrender the book to God and trust that everything would work out. Yet, to fully let go of my attachment to the book seemed like too gigantic of a step. Then my girlfriend asked me a question that totally caught me off guard. She said, "Can you surrender or let go of the book for just five minutes?" I hadn't thought of that before. It had always seemed like an all-or-nothing proposition. It was pretty obvious that, while in the middle of the desert, letting go of the book for five minutes was a reasonable enough thing to do. So I convinced my mind to just let go of the book "for five minutes." It let go. In fact, it let go for the rest of the trip. When I returned home from the desert, the first piece of mail I opened up was from a publisher who wanted to publish my book.

11. What are you painfully holding on to that you could surrender to God? As you receive an answer to this question, consider letting go of the entire situation. Imagine how that would feel.

12. Who do you know in need of love and prayers? If someone occurs to you, take the time to say a prayer or consider what act of love would be most appropriate.

Part II ★ Quick Contemplations

Frequently, we can't take time out of our busy lives to do even a brief meditation, yet we still want to see and experience things throughout our day from a more conscious or lofty perspective. I've found the following questions to be a powerful and practical way to quickly raise my consciousness. I used to try more complicated spiritual techniques, but I'd forget to use them when caught up in the details of life. So now I mostly stick with these simple questions. I sometimes put notes around my house to remind me to ask them throughout the day. Amazingly, in just ten seconds, the right question can completely alter how I perceive what's happening in my life.

Whether we are at a business meeting, changing a diaper, or answering the phone, a good question can redirect our attention in beneficial ways. As we get in the habit of asking ourselves such questions, we begin to experience the mundane activities of life from a more spiritual perspective.

When someone is doing something that's annoying or hurting you, to help yourself experience compassion, try these questions:

1. What hurt must this person have experienced in order to act this way?

2. Behind this person's act or facade, what is this person crying out for?

3. How is what this person is doing like something I do?

Sometimes asking other people a question can be scary, but it can change your life. As a freshman in college, I was extremely shy. To overcome my fear of rejection, I decided to ask ten women I'd never met if they would go out with me. As I approached the first woman, sweat poured from my forehead. When I said hello, my voice cracked. The woman saw the sweat dripping from my face and asked, "Are you all right?" She was worried that I was having an epileptic seizure. I assured her I was okay and proceeded to ask her if she'd go out with me. She nicely said she had a boyfriend, and we soon parted ways. I began to breathe again.

With each woman I asked, it got easier. By the seventh woman I approached, I was as loose as a goose. When I asked her if she wanted to go out with me, she said yes. Since I was anticipating rejection, I said, "Yes what?" She had to *convince* me she really wanted to go out with me! The next woman I asked out also said yes. And so did the next. Finally, I had so many dates lined up that I had to stop asking. My love life was never the same.

To help you express who you are and tune in to what you really want in a given situation, try asking the following questions:

4. If I weren't inhibited by fear, what would I want to say or do now?

5. Looking back on my life from my deathbed, what will I have felt good about doing in this situation?

6. If I knew I could not fail, what would I do?

To help you experience the joy of service and love, try these profound questions:

7. How can I truly be of service in this situation?

8. What would Jesus (or Buddha or your teacher) do in this situation?

9. What's the loving thing to say or do now?

10. How can I give my best right now?

11. If my heart could speak (or act), what would it say or do now?

When you're upset with your own behavior, try asking these questions as a way to feel compassion for yourself:

12. Behind my facade, what am I really crying out for?

13. What hurt was I feeling or have I experienced in the past that led me to act the way I did?

14. What can I do or tell myself now in order to feel better about myself?

A few years ago, I was teaching a psychology class at the local college. In this class, I was discussing how our minds are always asking the question, What is the meaning of this event or situation? Based on what we think an event means, we feel good or bad. For example, if we get fired from a job, we might think it means that our world has come to an end. On the other hand, we could choose to think it means that we now have the freedom to look for a new job that will be much better. With this parting example, I told the class to take a five-minute break.

During the break, a student whom I was friendly with told me he had something for me in his car. Once we walked to his car, he took a long time searching for this mysterious thing he was going to give me. Minute after minute passed, and he still couldn't find it. I became increasingly irritated, knowing that people were waiting for me back at the class. Each time I protested that I had to get back to class, the student would say, "Wait, just a second, I think I found it." He never did find "it," and I eventually walked back to class, thoroughly irritated by the inconvenience.

When I walked into class, I heard a resounding, "Surprise!" as students and friends had gathered to throw me a massive surprise birthday party. Suddenly, the student who had inconvenienced me at his car was seen in a new light. Although I had just been talking about it in class, I had not seen that there could be another meaning to his behavior. I had a good laugh at myself.

When situations go other than the way you want them to go, these questions can keep you positive and open to new learning:

15. *What else could this mean besides the negative meaning I've already attached to it?*

16. *What could I learn from this?*

17. *What could even be good about this?*

Finally, these questions can help you become more aware of how to let your heart soar amid the people and places you encounter every day:

18. *What could I bring to work that would help me be more in touch with a*

sense of my own heart and a sense of the sacred?

19. What could I do in my primary relationship(s) that would help me be more in touch with my own heart?

20. What could I do at home that would help me be more in touch with my spiritual essence?

Meditation on Living from the Heart

The following meditation is useful for letting go of thoughts and feelings that block your ability to live more fully from your heart. You'll have an opportunity to release any negative feelings you currently have and replace them with a heart-warming experience. As with the previous meditations, it can be helpful to record the following and play the tape back in a relaxing setting. Allow at least five minutes for the meditation.

Sit in a comfortable chair and take a couple of slow, deep breaths. Begin to focus on any feeling or thought in your body that feels unpleasant or uncomfortable in any way. Focus on the one feeling that is the most distressing. *(pause)* As you focus on this unpleasant sensation, notice the size of the uncomfortable feeling. Is it the size of a baseball, a basketball, or perhaps even bigger? *(pause)* Notice that along with the unpleasant feeling, there is a sense of your resisting the feeling. Allow yourself to relax your resistance and just feel what's there. *(pause)* Notice how as you relax your resistance, the feeling changes. *(pause)* How would you now describe the experience of this feeling? Does it feel warmer or cooler than the rest of your body? Does it feel heavier or lighter? Is it a constant sensation or does it pulse and fade? How would you describe the exact sensations of this feeling to someone who had never had a similar feeling? *(pause)* Notice how, as you just let the sensations *be* there, they change and become more pleasant. Notice how you become more relaxed and open to pleasant sensations and feelings expanding through your body. *(pause)* At this time, think of someone or something you really love, and as you picture this person or thing clearly in your mind, allow yourself to feel this warm love in your heart. *(pause)* With each and every breath, feel your heart area being filled with more light and love. *(pause)* Allow this pleasant feeling to expand throughout your entire body, filling every cell with a tingling sense of tenderness and vitality. *(pause)* When you're ready, you can slowly stretch, open your eyes, and enjoy your day.

14

THE SPIRITUAL
INTIMACY
EXPERIENCE

Love is a fruit in season at all times, and within reach of every hand.
Anyone may gather it and no limit is set.
—Mother Teresa

The word *intimacy* can be phonetically spelled out as "in-to-me-see." It could be said that the instructions for feeling intimacy are right within the word itself. When we drop our false personality and become our vulnerable self, in-to-me-see (intimacy) occurs. Within the word *spiritual* exists the words *spirit* and *ritual*. Once again, the way to feel spiritual is suggested by looking at the word.

We all crave to share spiritual intimacy with the people we care about, but the way to go about such a task is not always clear to us. By combining a "spirit ritual" with allowing someone to see deeply into our vulnerable feelings (in-to-me-see), true spiritual intimacy can occur.

In the spiritual intimacy experience, two people begin their journey by performing a simple spirit ritual together. They then proceed to disclose their answers to fifteen questions. The ritual you do to begin this process can be created by you, or you can begin by doing any of the following suggested rituals:

★ Find a comfortable and quiet place with your partner, light a candle, play some soft music, and look into each other's eyes for a couple of minutes before answering the fifteen questions.

★ Get comfortable with your partner, close your eyes, and pray in your preferred manner for what you hope to experience through answering the questions that follow.

★ Sit with your partner in a quiet place and silently contemplate what you most like about each other. After a couple minutes of reflection, proceed to answer the questions.

The following questions are designed to assist you in getting to know another person (either stranger, friend, or family member) on a fairly intimate level. They can be answered to whatever degree of self-disclosure you wish. Take as long as you like to answer. Once you're done, ask the same question of your partner, and let him or her respond. When you're asking the question, feel free to ask related questions that might further clarify or expand upon your partner's initial response. If a brief conversation naturally unfolds from your partner's response, that's perfectly alright as well.

I suggest *not* reading the questions ahead, so as to avoid mentally rehearsing or preparing yourself for what's to take place. Simply answer the questions as honestly and as thoroughly as you can. In seminars I lead, I've had hundreds of people pair up and answer these questions, resulting in a deep spiritual bond with the person they share the experience with. If you give this exercise enough time and sincerity, I think you'll find it to be a very satisfying and powerful experience.

1. When are you the happiest?

2. What is your greatest strength?

3. What is your greatest weakness?

4. What was the most difficult time in your life?

5. How do you keep yourself from being close to me?

6. When do you feel most affectionate?

7. What are you avoiding right now?

Once, while I was massaging my girlfriend's shoulders, I was surprised to hear her annoyedly say, "Would you please stop that? I don't like how you're always massaging me."

I was shocked. I thought giving a massage was a universal way of showing one's love. Yet to her it meant nothing but bother. I had assumed that the way *I* wanted to be loved would be the way *she* wanted to be loved. So I asked her, "When do you feel most loved by me?"

She said she feels most loved by me when we watch *Star Trek* on TV together or when I buy her flowers. So now we watch a lot of *Star Trek* shows, and I frequently buy her flowers. And she feels very loved. So do I, because now she knows to give me frequent massages. This one magical question has made our relationship more loving than I ever thought possible. Try it out with your partner.

8. What helps you to feel really loved?

9. What is one thing you regret having done?

10. How do you think I see you?

11. What is your heart longing for?

12. What do you consider to be your greatest accomplishment?

13. What was your first impression of me?

14. What do you like best about me?

15. What kind of person have you dreamed of becoming?

QUESTIONS
TO LIVE WITH

In the book of life's questions, the answers are not in the back.
—Charles Schultz

In the past thirty years, two contradictory trends have accelerated. First, there has been an increasing level of material distraction as evidenced by ringing phones, incoming faxes, endless junk mail, and sixty channels of TV. This trend is colliding with our desire to seek deeper meaning, purpose, and peace in our lives. Only one thing can be certain: In the next decade, there will be more distractions available than ever before. Even today, the average American spends more than four hours a day watching television. In our increasingly complex and noisy world, it takes a sincere intention to ask and try to answer the "big questions." And in a world that promises instant solutions and gratification, it can be difficult to keep searching for better and better answers.

In my pursuit to stay aligned with a deeper sense of purpose, over the years I've selected a half-dozen questions I ask myself at least once a week. I've found that when I ask myself these questions, and listen to my intuition, the answers I receive help me to stay centered and on track. The questions that work best for me in this regard are the following:

1. What can I do this week to have fun and be aligned with my sense of purpose?

2. What could I feel grateful for in my life?

3. How can I use the gifts I've been given to better serve people?

4. What can I do to take better care of myself?

5. Is there anything I'm doing that is hurting myself, other people, or steering me off course?

6. What do I need to know or do to take my next step forward for personal and spiritual growth?

If these questions resonate with you, try them as weekly or monthly reminders. Feel free to come up with different inquiries that may be more suitable for your purposes. Write them on a note card so they'll always be close at hand. Experiment with various questions to see which ones serve you the best.

My hope is that the questions in this book become your lasting, lifelong friends. In my own life, I have found that the search for answers brings me an ever-deepening sense of purpose and peace. When asking these questions of the people I love, I have been blessed with fascinating conversations, deeper intimacy, and ideas that have greatly benefited my life. I encourage you to share this book and these questions with your friends and family. I hope the answers you find along the way bring you an abundance of beauty, joy, and love.

RESOURCES FOR
FURTHER EXPLORATION

The measure of a person's knowledge is the actions they take.
—Saint Francis of Assisi

The books, movies, and resource guides in this section can help inspire, educate, and transform you in meaningful ways. Perhaps they will help you find even better answers to life's big questions.

Recommended Movies

In seminars I lead across the country, I've asked hundreds of people to list the movies they have found to be the most inspiring to them. Below, in alphabetical order, are the top twenty picks I've received.

1. *Babette's Feast*
2. *Being There*
3. *Brother Sun, Sister Moon*
4. *Chariots of Fire*
5. *Dances with Wolves*
6. *Dead Poets Society*
7. *Forrest Gump*
8. *Gandhi*
9. *Gone with the Wind*
10. *Groundhog Day*
11. *Harold and Maude*
12. *Hearts and Souls*
13. *Like Water for Chocolate*
14. *Midnight Express*
15. *Mindwalk*
16. *Out of Africa*
17. *Philadelphia*

18. *The Razor's Edge*
19. *Resurrection*
20. *Schindler's List*

Recommended Books

As with the movies, I've asked hundreds of people to write down the most inspiring and/or helpful books they've read. In alphabetical order are the top twenty picks.

Book Title	Author
1. *Another Heart in His Hand*	J. J. Gold
2. *A Return to Love*	Marianne Williamson
3. *Bridges to Heaven*	Jonathan Robinson
4. *Bringers of the Dawn*	Barbara Marciniak

Spiritual Resource Guides

1. *Fodor's Healthy Escapes: 243 Resorts and Retreats Where You Can Get Fit, Feel Good, and Find Yourself*

2. *The Spiritual Seeker's Guide: The Complete Source for Religions and Spiritual Groups of the World* (compiled by Steven Sadleir)

3. *Transformative Adventures, Vacations, and Retreats* (compiled by John Benson)

4. *Values & Visions* (bimonthly), *Values & Visions Circles Newsletter,* and a catalog listing over 300 discussion guides to movies, videos and books, available from: Cultural Information Service, P.O. Box 786, Madison Square Station, New York, NY 10159; (800)929-4857.

About the Author

Jonathan Robinson is a psychotherapist, workshop leader, and professional speaker living in Santa Barbara, California. He has spent more than twenty years studying the most practical and powerful methods for psychological and spiritual growth. He is also the editor of the book *Bridges to Heaven: How Well-Known Seekers Define and Deepen Their Connection with God*.

If you would like a free catalog of Jonathan's audio and videotapes, or more information about his workshops and public talks, please contact:

Jonathan Robinson
P.O. Box 1501
Santa Barbara, CA 93102
Fax: (805) 967-4128

Other inspirational titles from Conari Press that address life's "big questions" include:

Random Acts of Kindness

Kids' Random Acts of Kindness

More Random Acts of Kindness

Dancing Up the Moon:
A Woman's Guide to Creating Traditions that Bring Sacredness to Daily Life

Keys to the Open Gate:
A Woman's Spirituality Sourcebook

A Grateful Heart:
Daily Blessings for the Evening Meal from Buddha to the Beatles

True Love:
How to Make Your Relationship Sweeter, Deeper & More Passionate

Heart & Soul:
Living the Joy, Truth & Beauty of Your Intimate Relationship

Conari Press, established in 1987, publishes books on topics ranging from spirituality and women's history to sexuality and personal growth. Our main goal is to publish quality books that will make a difference in people's lives—both how we feel about ourselves and how we relate to one another.

Our readers are our most important resource, and we value your input, suggestions, and ideas. We'd love to hear from you—after all, we are publishing books for you!

For a complete catalog or to get on our mailing list, please contact us at:

CONARI PRESS
2550 Ninth Street, Suite 101
Berkeley, CA 94710
Phone: (800) 685-9595